Partners In PERU

Written By

Barbara Massey
and Sylvia DeLoach

Illustrations By

Amy Giles

New Hope Publishers
Birmingham, AL

New Hope Publishers
P.O. Box 12065
Birmingham, AL 35202-2065

© 1998 by New Hope Publishers
All rights reserved. First printing 1998
Printed in Hong Kong

Dewey Decimal Classification: J 985
Subject Headings: Peru—Children's Literature
                        Peru—Social Life and Customs

Cover design and illustration by Amy Giles

ISBN: 1-56309-258-1
N987105 • 0798 • 3M1

To order products from New Hope Publishers or for a free catalog,
call 1-800-968-7301. Also, visit our website at newhopepubl.com.

Mrs. Collins put down her briefcase, kicked off her shoes, and called to her daughter, "Christina, do I have a surprise for you!"

Christina turned off her computer and ran to find her mom. After hugging her, Christina asked, "Okay, Mom. What's the big surprise?"

Christina's mother started looking through the mail as she said, "Well, remember I promised you a long time ago that I would take you on one of my trips with me?"

"Yes," Christina said as she watched her mother's smile get bigger and bigger. "Really, Mom? You mean I'm finally going to get to go somewhere with you?"

Nodding as she answered, Mrs. Collins said, "How does a two-week trip to Peru sound for a way to spend your Christmas holidays?"

"Peru!" Christina practically yelled. "Do you really mean it, Mom? I have to go call my friends! Right now!"

That night after dinner, Mrs. Collins opened her briefcase and pulled out a folder of papers. Her travel agency was sending her to Peru to explore sights tourists might be interested in. "Christina," her mom said as they sat on the couch in the den, "not very long ago Peru was voted the best tourist destination by *The Observer*, a London newspaper, and also at the International Expo Fair in Hong Kong. My travel agency thinks we should become more familiar with Peru and offer travel packages to our clients. I think this is a perfect assignment for a mother-daughter team."

"Me, too, Mom. Let's get started," Christina said excitedly.

That night, Christina got out her passport and laid it on the table beside her bed. She drifted off to sleep thinking about getting her very first stamp on her passport.

In the next few weeks, every afternoon and every weekend Christina and her mom thought of nothing but Peru and getting ready for their great adventure together.

One Saturday when they were getting their clothes ready for the trip, Christina said, "Mom, I can take my new sweaters and jeans."

"Well, Christina, you might want to think about that," said her mom, "because guess what? It's going to be summer there."

"I already love this," Christina giggled as she pulled out shorts and T-shirts instead. "We're going to have our first summertime Christmas!"

Soon the big day came. Christina and her mom arrived at the airport in Miami, Florida, to board the plane for Lima, Peru. As Christina settled into her seat by the window, she snuggled up to her mother and said, "Mom, this is going to be the best surprise ever."

Six hours later, as the jet hovered over Lima, the capital city, Christina looked out the window to see where their adventure would begin. "We're here, Mom!" she said as their plane set down at Jorge Chávez [HOR hay CHAH vehs] Airport.

In no time at all, Christina and Mrs. Collins went through customs and exchanged their American dollars for Peruvian *nuevos soles* [NWEH vohs SOHL ehs]. "Now to find a ride to our hotel," Mrs. Collins said as they gathered their luggage.

As their taxi made its way from the airport into Lima, Christina's eyes opened wide to take in all the surroundings. "Mom, I knew that Peru would be different from America, but I didn't know that it would be this different."

"Well, I've thought the same thing about every place I've traveled for our agency," said Mom. "But, that's what's neat about traveling. Each place and culture *is* different."

My Name Is:

In Peru, as in other Hispanic countries, names have three parts: 1) given name, 2) father's last name, 3) mother's maiden name. So, a young boy may be named Pedro (given name), Suárez (father's last name), Durán (mother's maiden name).

Standing in their hotel room later, Christina and her mother took their first long look at the view from their hotel window. "Mom, isn't it strange to see people on the beach in December?" Christina asked, as she looked out at the beautiful view of the Pacific Ocean.

"Well, like you said, Christina, it's going to be a warm Christmas this year. Now, let's get unpacked and ready for bed," said Mom. "We've got a long day tomorrow. And since you are my partner on this business trip, you will have to be ready early to meet Señora Barra with me."

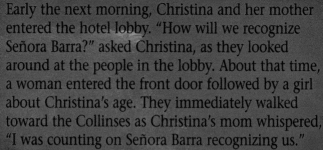

Early the next morning, Christina and her mother entered the hotel lobby. "How will we recognize Señora Barra?" asked Christina, as they looked around at the people in the lobby. About that time, a woman entered the front door followed by a girl about Christina's age. They immediately walked toward the Collinses as Christina's mom whispered, "I was counting on Señora Barra recognizing us."

Seeing Señora Barra's name tag, Mrs. Collins said, "Buenos días," in her very best Spanish as she extended her hand to Señora Barra. "This is my daughter Christina I wrote you about."

"And this is my daughter María Elena," replied Señora Barra. "I thought since they are about the same age they both might enjoy coming with us as we explore Peru together."

Christina and María Elena exchanged smiles and Christina thought to herself, *This is going to be even more fun than I imagined.*

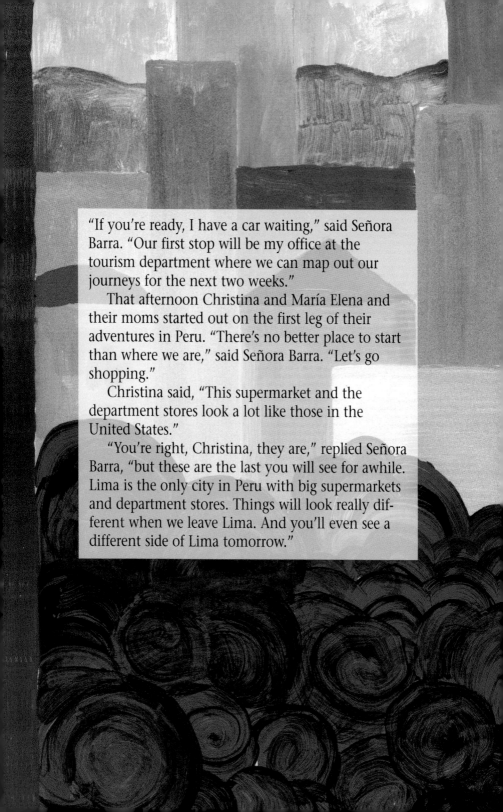

"If you're ready, I have a car waiting," said Señora Barra. "Our first stop will be my office at the tourism department where we can map out our journeys for the next two weeks."

That afternoon Christina and María Elena and their moms started out on the first leg of their adventures in Peru. "There's no better place to start than where we are," said Señora Barra. "Let's go shopping."

Christina said, "This supermarket and the department stores look a lot like those in the United States."

"You're right, Christina, they are," replied Señora Barra, "but these are the last you will see for awhile. Lima is the only city in Peru with big supermarkets and department stores. Things will look really different when we leave Lima. And you'll even see a different side of Lima tomorrow."

The next morning Señora Barra and María Elena picked up Christina and her mother at the hotel. "As I told you yesterday, we're going to see a very different part of Lima today. Everybody ready?"

Christina slung her backpack over her shoulder and jumped into the car beside María Elena. "I'm glad you're learning English at your school just like I'm learning Spanish at mine," said Christina.

"Yes," said María Elena. "We can practice as we travel."

As the car made its way from the center of Lima to outlying areas, Señora Barra talked about life in Lima.

"Earning a living in Peru is not easy for most people," she said. "Farming rice, wheat, and potatoes is what most of the mountain people do. Few Peruvians own cars. In fact, walking is the main form of transportation."

By this time, when Christina looked out the car window the scenery had changed from the city to something very different. "What's that, Señora Barra?" Christina asked.

"Well," replied Señora Barra, "when times get hard and families cannot make a living from the land, they come to the big city to find work. When they get to Lima, they begin to try to find people who might have moved from their area—maybe even relatives. Then they move in with them. Conditions can get very crowded, so they begin to look for more space. Any public land is up for grabs. Christina, what you just asked about is the beginning of such a new community. It's called a *pueblo joven* [PWEH bloh HOH vehn]. In English you would say *young town*."

"You mean those four straw mats?" asked Christina.

"Yes," continued Señora Barra. "Very often a pueblo joven is started by four straw mats that serve as a house. Little by little, the people in this pueblo joven begin to form a community. They start businesses and build homes. Because of these new communities, Lima is getting bigger and bigger. It is growing from the center of the city out over the sand dunes."

Mrs. Collins and Christina continued to explore Lima with their guides for several days, until the morning arrived when they would take their first journey away from the city. Señora Barra and Mrs. Collins had decided on a journey that would follow the southern route, a common trip combining air, rail, and road travel. Their first journey would be by rail. As they boarded the train for Arequipa [ah reh KEE pah], Christina said, "My first train ride," when she settled into her place by María Elena.

"Have you ever seen a volcano?" asked María Elena.

"No," answered Christina. "My first volcano!"

Señora Barra said, "Arequipa, our destination for today, stands in a beautiful valley at the foot of El Misti—your first volcano, Christina."

Señora Barra turned to Mrs. Collins and said, "When you begin to put together your travel package for your agency, there is one package that will appeal to the adventurous traveler. Tourists may actually climb El Misti. It takes all day to reach the Monte Blanco shelter at 4,800 meters. Those who desire to reach the top may spend the night at Monte Blanco. An early start the next morning will allow the climbers to reach the summit before the mists make it impossible to enjoy the view."

Christina exclaimed, "Wow! There it is! It looks like a giant snowcapped cone!"

When the train pulled in to Arequipa, Señora Barra led the way to the Plaza de Armas, a plaza beautifully laid out with palm trees, gardens, and a fountain among the businesses and restaurants. "María Elena," said Señora Barra, "you and Christina may explore the gardens and enjoy the fountain while Mrs. Collins and I stop by the tourist office on the Plaza."

"Stay together, and we'll meet you at the fountain in 30 minutes," the mothers called as María Elena took Christina's hand and led her toward the gardens.

The time in Arequipa passed quickly. Their next tourist attraction was Lake Titicaca.

"Lake Titicaca is the largest lake in South America," said Señora Barra as the train rumbled along.

"Can we go across it?" asked Christina.

"Christina, I will be able to plan tours for travelers," answered her mom, "but we will not be stopping there this time."

Lake Titicaca is the largest lake in South America.

"But, Christina, if we did cross it today, do you realize you would be going into another country?" asked Señora Barra.

"Really?" asked Christina, puzzled.

"Yes," said María Elena, "half of the lake is in Peru and half is in Bolivia."

"And, Christina, remember the mats in the young town at Lima?" asked Señora Barra. "Well, they may have been made from reeds that grow in this lake. They're called *totora* reeds. The people who live at Lake Titicaca are known for the mats and boats they make from totora reeds."

Christina still couldn't believe that she was spending her Christmas holidays traveling in a new country. *And,* she thought to herself as she looked at María Elena, *I got a new friend for Christmas this year.*

When the four new friends arrived in Cuzco, they were ready to explore the ancient Inca capital. Señora Barra pointed out that most people are confused about the Incas. "The Incas were the rulers, not the people. And, Christina, there's a new word for you to learn—*Quechua* [KEH chwah].

"Quechua," repeated Christina, trying to say it exactly like Señora Barra. "What does that mean?"

"That is what the people are called. Quechuas were ruled by the Incas long ago."

"And didn't you tell me, Señora Barra, that almost every street has remains of Inca walls, arches, and doorways?" asked Mrs. Collins.

"Sí," answered Señora Barra, "and they are over 800 years old."

"I've got to see those," Christina chimed in. "That's really old."

In their walk through Cuzco, Señora Barra led them to the Plaza San Blas. "Many of our villages are known for their local crafts," she said.

"Can we buy some, Mom?" asked Christina.

"Certainly. What great Christmas presents for our friends at home," answered Mrs. Collins. Señora Barra led the group. They found woodworkers on almost every street. "We must stop here," said Señora Barra. "This man is one of our leading craftsmen. He makes biblical figures from plaster, wheat flour, and potatoes."

No sooner had Señora Barra said the word *potatoes*, than Christina echoed her, "Potatoes! Did you say potatoes?"

"That's exactly what I said, Christina," replied Señora Barra. "I'll bet you didn't know the potato originated in Peru. In fact, the International Potato Center is located in Lima."

"Wow!" said Christina. "I thought potatoes were originally from the US."

As Christina and her mom looked at the figures, she knew exactly what she wanted to buy—a beautiful nativity made from plaster, wheat flour, and potatoes. "We can put this in our hotel room, Mom, to celebrate Christmas."

"And what a wonderful reminder it will always be of the Christmas we spent in Peru," answered Mrs. Collins.

"Before we leave Cuzco," Señora Barra said, "you must experience shopping at the *mercado*. This open-air market has everything from clothing to hardware to fresh fruits and vegetables."

As the four travelers stopped at a mercado, Mrs. Collins offered, "Let us buy some fruit to carry with us on the next part of our trip."

Peruvians are known for their skills with cloth and ceramics. Craftsmen make dolls and toy llamas, and weave rugs and clothing from colorful fabrics, often made from llama wool.

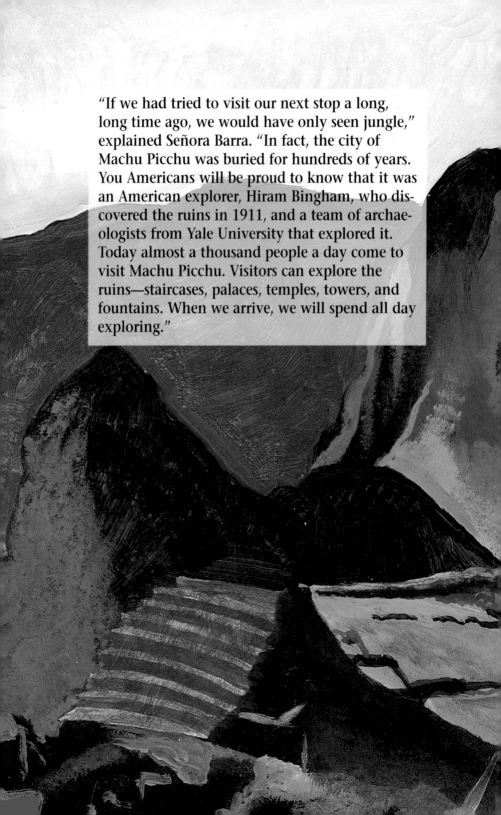

"If we had tried to visit our next stop a long, long time ago, we would have only seen jungle," explained Señora Barra. "In fact, the city of Machu Picchu was buried for hundreds of years. You Americans will be proud to know that it was an American explorer, Hiram Bingham, who discovered the ruins in 1911, and a team of archaeologists from Yale University that explored it. Today almost a thousand people a day come to visit Machu Picchu. Visitors can explore the ruins—staircases, palaces, temples, towers, and fountains. When we arrive, we will spend all day exploring."

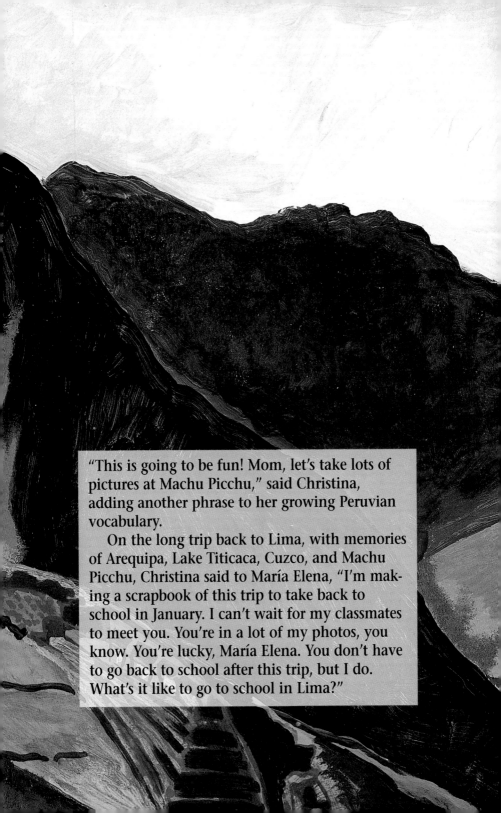

"This is going to be fun! Mom, let's take lots of pictures at Machu Picchu," said Christina, adding another phrase to her growing Peruvian vocabulary.

On the long trip back to Lima, with memories of Arequipa, Lake Titicaca, Cuzco, and Machu Picchu, Christina said to María Elena, "I'm making a scrapbook of this trip to take back to school in January. I can't wait for my classmates to meet you. You're in a lot of my photos, you know. You're lucky, María Elena. You don't have to go back to school after this trip, but I do. What's it like to go to school in Lima?"

For several minutes, María Elena told Christina about her school. "We have both private and national schools. I go to a national school. We don't have very many teaching materials and supplies. In fact, my parents have to buy my textbooks. We memorize a lot. I spend a lot of time copying my work into a tablet and then I memorize it."

"That is different," said Christina.

María Elena went on, "I started school in kindergarten."

"Me, too," said Christina. "Tell me more."

"Well, I have to wear a uniform. We all do," said María Elena.

"You mean you wear the same thing every day?" asked Christina. "What does it look like?"

"I wear a gray skirt, a white shirt, gray knee socks, gray sweater, and black shoes," María Elena continued. "What do you wear to school?"

"Some schools in America have uniforms, but we don't wear them at my school," Christina replied. "I just thought of one way we are alike, though. Soccer!"

In Peru, soccer is the most popular sport.

"We call it *fútbol*," María Elena answered. "I play on a team."

"Me, too," replied Christina, grinning.

Upon their return to the hotel in Lima on Christmas Eve, Christina said, "I feel like we are at home, Mom." She carefully unwrapped the nativity figures and placed them on a table by the window overlooking the Pacific Ocean.

"And we have another adventure awaiting us tonight," replied her mom. "We've been invited to join the Barra family for a church service tonight at mid-night."

"And María Elena said we are going to her house afterwards for a special treat," said Christina. "I guess this is one Christmas Eve I get to stay up really late!"

After a beautiful Christmas Eve service, the Collinses joined the Barras in their home. The special treat turned out to be something Christina loved. There was hot chocolate and *paneton* [pah neh TOHN]—a yeast bread with bits of dried fruit. Christina was amazed at how large María Elena's family was. She not only had brothers and sisters, but also an aunt, uncle, cousins, and grandparents living in the home. As the Collinses left for the hotel, Christina said to Señora Barra, "That was fun to celebrate with so many people. I love your family."

Señora Barra replied, "That is good, because we all want you to come back New Year's Eve."

All the next week, Christina and her mom continued to enjoy their trip. Mrs. Collins spent some time working out the details for package tours to the places they had visited. After getting their first rolls of film developed, Christina began work on her scrapbook. She even made her own travel package. When she showed it to her mom, she said, "Since you and I are partners in this adventure, you may be able to use some of my ideas in your travel package."

"You know, Christina, we saw a lot, but there's so much yet that we didn't get to visit. Peru is a big country. It's the third largest country in South America."

"Well, that just means we have to come back, Mom," said Christina. "Next time let's ask Señora Barra and María Elena to take us to the Amazon jungle."

"The Amazon River is definitely on my list," replied Mrs. Collins. "I wonder what kind of adventure we could have by boat on the Amazon River? I'm also interested in the Andes. It's one of the world's major mountain ranges. Travel partner, let's remember to ask Señora Barra how to travel to these locations."

Before long it was New Year's Eve. Señora Barra arranged to pick up Mrs. Collins and Christina at the hotel. "I'm glad you could be ready this early," she said, as she made the drive to her home. "It's difficult to drive on the streets on New Year's Eve."

"Why, because there's more traffic?" asked Mrs. Collins.

"No," replied Señora Barra, "it's because of the smoke."

"Smoke?" asked Christina. "Is there a fire?"

"There will be—many fires," answered Señora Barra. "It is our custom in Peru to burn old tires and all sorts of rubbish on New Year's Eve. The fires represent the passing of the old year."

The Barra family greeted their guests with "Feliz Año Nuevo [feh LEES ah nyoh NWEH voh]!"

"Ummm, something smells good," said Christina as she followed María Elena to the kitchen.

"It's *lomo saltado*, my favorite," said María Elena.

In the kitchen, Christina and María Elena watched the grandmother cut steak into small bits. She cooked it with onions, tomato, and pepper. When this mixture was done, she added French-fried potatoes. At dinner that evening, this was served over rice.

"Mom, I hope you'll make this when we get home," commented Christina. "It's delicious."

"Wait until you try the dessert," whispered María Elena. "You'll really want your Mom to make that in America."

The national dish of Peru is ceviche [seh VEE cheh], a spicy dish of onions and seafood. Fish is soaked in lime juice, then onion, hot peppers, and coriander are added to complete the dish.

When Christina tasted the *pionono* [pyoh NOH noh], she knew María Elena was right. This jelly roll dessert was filled with *manjar blanca* [mahn HAHR BLAHN kah], a thickened caramelized milk filling. "Yummm," said Christina, as she thanked Señora Barra and the grandmother for such a good New Year's Eve meal.

As everyone sat around talking after dinner, Christina thought about all the fun she and María Elena had had together in Peru. *I can't believe I'll be going home the day after tomorrow,* she thought to herself. *I think time passes faster in Peru.*

"Grandmother," María Elena said pleadingly, "I know that Christina has learned a lot about Peru these last two weeks, but there's one thing she hasn't gotten to do. She hasn't heard you tell the llama story! Please tell it, Grandmother. Please?"

Everyone settled in as Grandmother began to tell the old Peruvian story.

"Well, it goes like this," began grandmother as her eyes twinkled.

"Once upon a time there lived a farmer and his family. Their most prized possession was a llama. He worked each day carrying heavy loads from the fields. The farmer was very kind to his llama. He wanted the llama to have the very best grass to eat. One day he took the llama to a green field. He told the llama to eat. But, the llama would not.

"For several days the farmer took the llama to the green field, but the llama refused to eat. Instead, the llama began to cry. The farmer was very surprised to see his llama cry. He was even more sur-prised when he heard the llama speak.

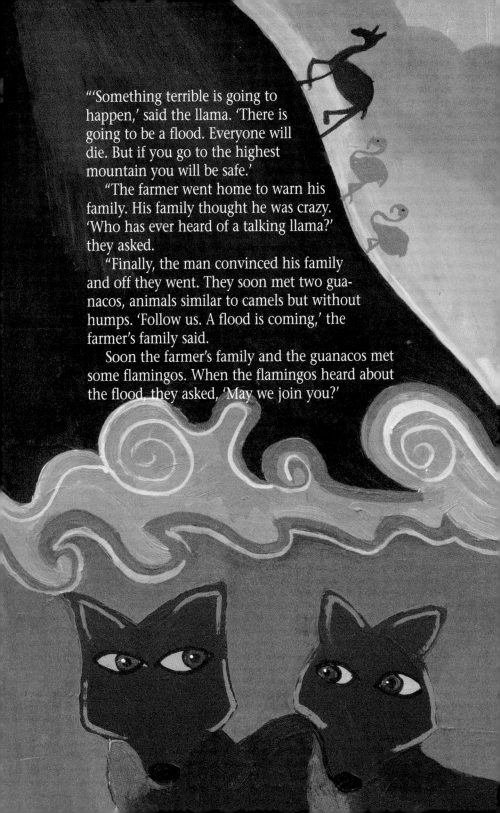

"'Something terrible is going to happen,' said the llama. 'There is going to be a flood. Everyone will die. But if you go to the highest mountain you will be safe.'

"The farmer went home to warn his family. His family thought he was crazy. 'Who has ever heard of a talking llama?' they asked.

"Finally, the man convinced his family and off they went. They soon met two guanacos, animals similar to camels but without humps. 'Follow us. A flood is coming,' the farmer's family said.

Soon the farmer's family and the guanacos met some flamingos. When the flamingos heard about the flood, they asked, 'May we join you?'

"And the llama said, 'Come along!'

"The waters were rapidly rising behind them, but the llama and his friends kept climbing. They were joined by a puma and her cubs, two chinchillas, and two condors. The last animals they met were a family of foxes. When the llama tried to warn them, the foxes did not believe him. They refused to go along.

"Finally, the llama and his followers arrived on the mountain top. They saw the high water below. They also saw the foxes running up the mountain. "'Hurry,' said the llama. The foxes made it, but their tails hung into the water."

María Elena's grandmother paused and looked over at the two girls. "That's why, even today, foxes' tails are black where the dark waters touched them in their scramble up the mountain. Today the people of Peru enjoy thinking about this talking llama. That's why we put bells and ribbons on our llamas. We like to take them to green fields to eat. Sometimes a farmer will play a flute while his llama is eating. It seems like the llama is moving his ears in time to the music. But, do you know what, girls? Not a single llama has talked again!"

As Christina and her mother left the Barra home that evening, Christina turned to the grandmother and said, "That was a great llama story. The next time I see a llama in our zoo, I'll think about how funny it would be to hear him talking."

Two days later as their plane left the runway and climbed higher and higher, Christina asked, "How did I do, Mom?"

"You make a great partner," said Mom, smiling. "What are you thinking?" she asked, as Christina gazed out the window watching Lima grow smaller below.

"I'm thinking I would make a great tour guide for one of those tours you are planning," replied Christina.

"Sí," said Mrs. Collins. "I think so, too."